D1348834

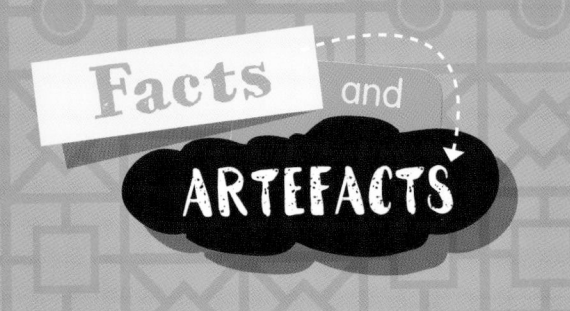

MAYAS AND INCAS

Anita Croy

W

FRANKLIN WATTS

LONDON • SYDNEY

Published in Great Britain in 2018 by
The Watts Publishing Group

Copyright © 2018 Brown Bear Books Ltd

For Brown Bear Books Ltd:
Managing Editor: Tim Cooke
Children's Publisher: Anne O'Daly
Editorial Director: Lindsey Lowe
Design Manager: Keith Davis
Designer and Illustrator: Supriya Sahai
Picture Manager: Sophie Mortimer

Concept development: Square and Circus/
Brown Bear Books Ltd

ISBN 978 1 4451 6187 7

Printed in Malaysia

Franklin Watts
An imprint of
Hachette Children's Group
Part of the Watts Publishing Group
Carmelite House
50 Victoria Embankment
London EC4Y 0DZ

An Hachette UK company
www.hachette.co.uk
www.franklinwatts.co.uk

FSC
www.fsc.org
MIX
Paper from
responsible sources
FSC® C137506

CONTENTS

MAYAS AND INCAS

The Mayas and Incas were important civilisations. The Mayas were in Central America, while the Incas were in South America. Both built powerful empires and left behind objects that provide evidence of how they lived.

MAYA AND INCA HISTORY

The Maya empire of Central America was at its peak between the sixth and tenth centuries CE. This is during the later part of what is called the Classical Period. The Mayas built cities and developed their own writing system. The centre of Mayan culture moved north around 900. No one really knows why.

In the twelfth century, the Incas began to build an empire in the Andes mountains of what is now Peru. In just 400 years they built the largest empire in the Americas. In 1532, the empire was invaded by Spanish conquistadors, who killed the last Inca emperor in 1572.

This painting shows the Inca emperor Atahualpa. He was killed by Spanish conquistadors in 1533.

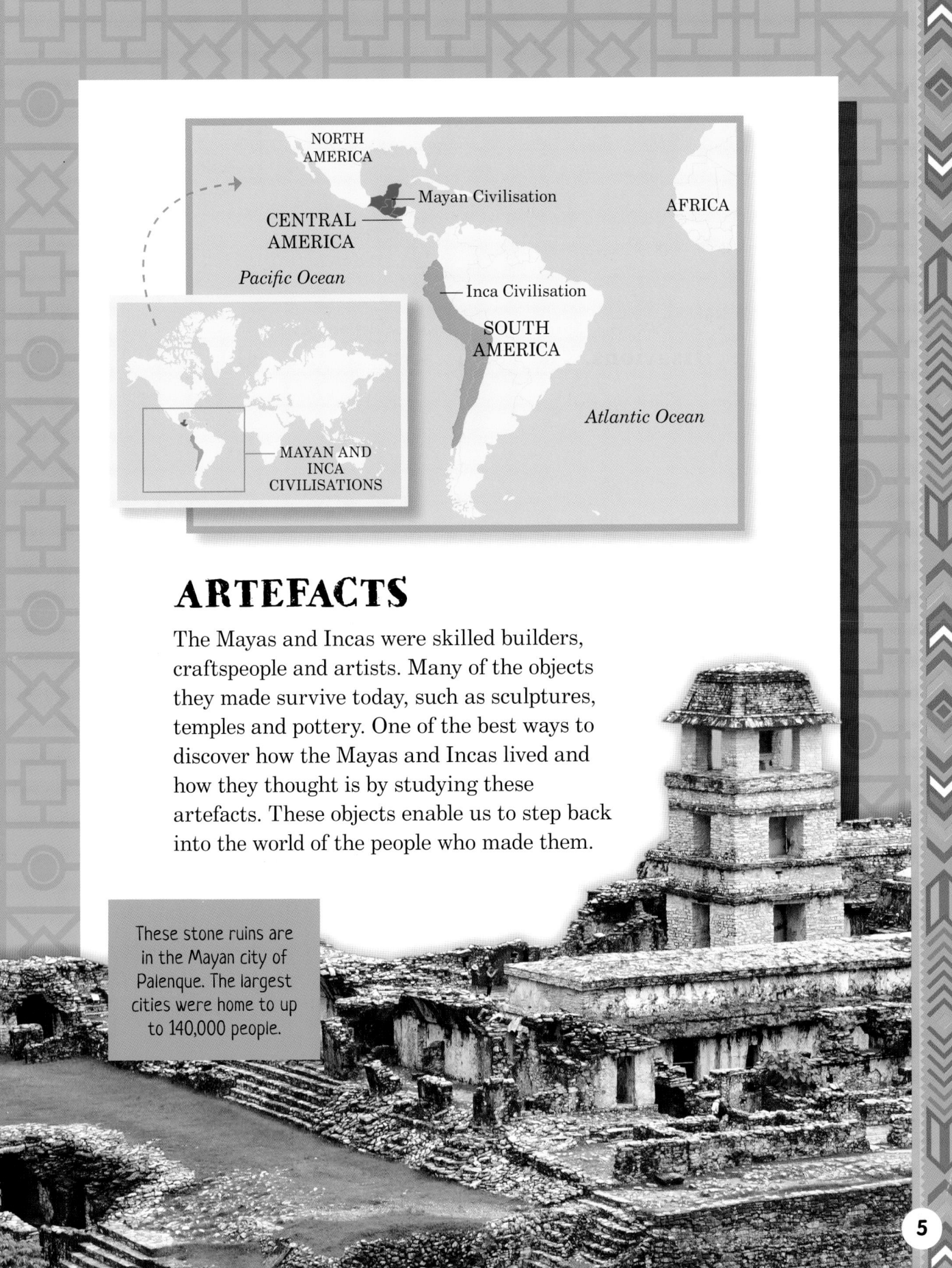

NORTH
AMERICA

Mayan Civilisation

CENTRAL
AMERICA

AFRICA

Pacific Ocean

Inca Civilisation

SOUTH
AMERICA

Atlantic Ocean

MAYAN AND
INCA
CIVILISATIONS

ARTEFACTS

The Mayas and Incas were skilled builders, craftspeople and artists. Many of the objects they made survive today, such as sculptures, temples and pottery. One of the best ways to discover how the Mayas and Incas lived and how they thought is by studying these artefacts. These objects enable us to step back into the world of the people who made them.

These stone ruins are in the Mayan city of Palenque. The largest cities were home to up to 140,000 people.

THE LAND OF THE MAYAS

The Mayan civilisation began around 1000 BCE in the lowlands of Central America and southeast Mexico. The Mayas controlled their empire from cities such as Tikal, Palenque and Copán. Over the 2,600-year history of the empire, the different cities rose and fell in power.

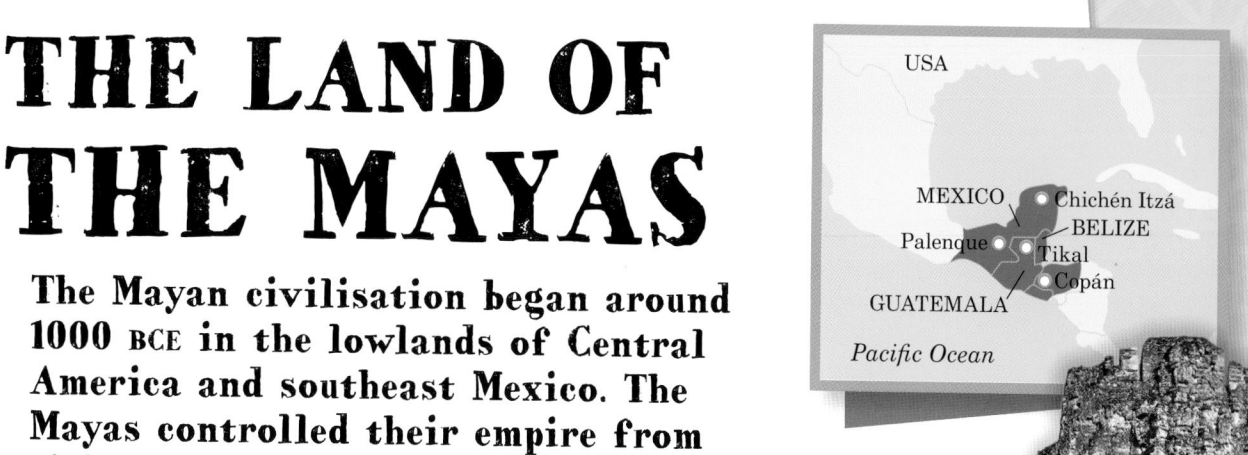

USA
MEXICO
Chichén Itzá
Palenque
BELIZE
Tikal
Copán
GUATEMALA
Pacific Ocean

☞ THE FACTS

- The Mayas were expert astronomers and mathematicians.
- They invented their own form of writing.
- The Mayas worshipped many different gods associated with the Sun, rain and nature.
- Classical Mayan culture collapsed suddenly in around CE 900. No one knows why.
- After the classicial civilisation ended, the Mayas moved north and founded a new civilisation at Chichén Itzá. It lasted until the sixteenth century.

The Temple of the Great Jaguar was built at one end of the Great Plazza in Tikal in about CE 732.

CODEX

The Mayas recorded their history in 'books' of cloth made from tree bark folded into sheets. These books were called codices.

The Mayas used codices to record details about their history and their religious beliefs. When Spanish conquerors arrived in the sixteenth century, they destroyed any codices they found. They were trying to wipe out all evidence of the Mayas' non-Christian religion. Today only four codices survive. The best preserved of them is the Dresden Codex. It shows the observations of Mayan astronomers, including the cycles of the Moon and Sun.

The Mayas built their temples as stepped pyramids, like this one in Chichén Itzá.

The shrine on top of the nine-stepped pyramid was built to cover the tomb of a ruler of Tikal.

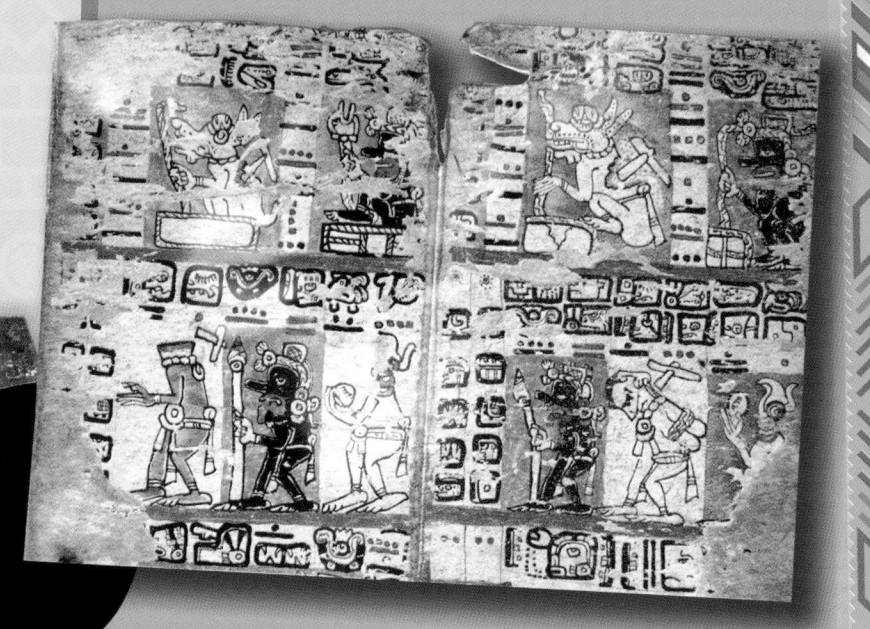

The Dresden Codex was created around the thirteenth century CE. It is the oldest book in the Americas.

MAYAN CITY-STATES

The Mayan empire was divided into city-states, such as Tikal and Palenque. The city-states often fought each other for dominance. Each city-state had its own ruler. The Mayas believed these kings communicated with the gods. They thought the kings became gods when they died.

This carving from Palenque shows King Pakal sitting on his throne. Pakal ruled from CE 615 to 683.

☞ THE FACTS

Each main city had a central complex with stone palaces, temples, plazas and a court for playing the sacred ballgame, *pitz*. Some temples were tall step-sided pyramids, which only priests could enter. Ordinary people lived in wooden homes around the outside of the city. Their homes have largely disappeared. Archaeologists are certain that the stone ruins of many Mayan cities still wait to be discovered beneath the jungle foliage of Mexico, Guatemala and Belize.

These royal temple tombs are in the centre of Palenque. They include the tomb of King Pakal.

DEATH MASK

The seventh-century CE ruler Pakal was the greatest king of the Mayan city-state of Palenque.

During his reign, Pakal the Great turned Palenque from an unimportant city to a great power. When he died in CE 683, he had ruled for longer than any other Mayan king. This jade mask is a death mask. It was placed over the dead king's face. Pakal was buried in a decorated sarcophagus, which was placed inside his tomb beneath the Temple of the Inscriptions. The sides of his burial chamber were decorated with sculptures and relief carvings. They showed Pakal turning into a god after his death.

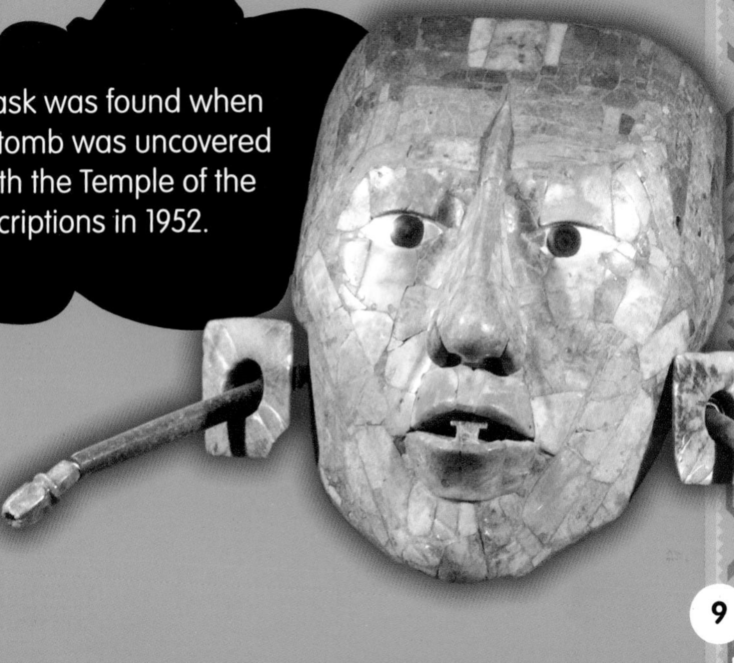

This mask was found when Pakal's tomb was uncovered beneath the Temple of the Inscriptions in 1952.

WRITING

The Mayas developed the earliest-known system of writing in the Americas. They used symbols called glyphs that were carved into stone or written on sheets of paper made from bark. The Mayas were also skilled mathematicians. Their number system used base 20 (we use base 10). They had characters for zero (a shell shape), one (a dot) and five (a bar).

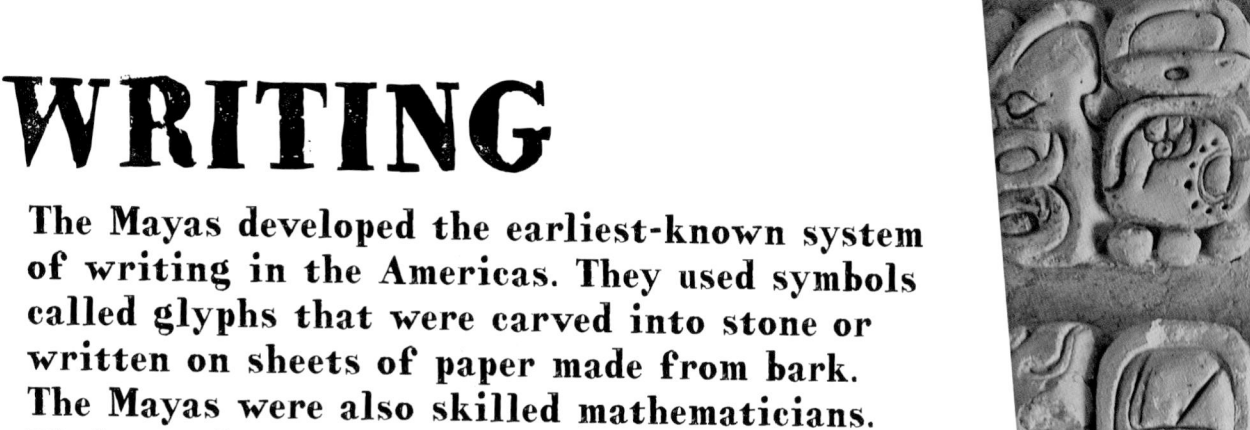

Glyphs were arranged in blocks. Each block contained two vertical columns of symbols.

Carved Mayan glyphs were usually painted to make them easier to read.

👉 THE FACTS

- The Maya created around 850 different glyphs.
- Each glyph stood for a word, part of a word, a sound, an idea or a number.
- Historians today can interpret about 90 per cent of Mayan glyphs.
- Mayan writing was carved on stelae (standing stone slabs), stone lintels, sculptures and pottery. It was also painted in codices (see page 7).

PAKAL'S LIFE

Preserved in the Temple of the Inscriptions at Palenque, these stone glyphs are part of a long account of the life of King Pakal.

The account was carved during the king's lifetime and celebrates his achievements. The original glyphs were painted red, but the colour has faded over time. The temple also contains three inscribed stone tablets that tell archaeologists a lot about Mayan religion. The Mayas believed time moved in cycles. That meant events in the past would be repeated on the same date in the future.

Mayan buildings were carved with glyphs and geometric designs.

Some glyphs, like these demons, were pictures of the objects they described.

THE SACRED BALLGAME

Mayan religion was based on keeping the gods happy. Each city had a ball court where athletes played a sacred ballgame to honour the gods. Sometimes the winning captain was killed for the gods, which was considered a great honour.

The ballgame was played on a court shaped like a capital I.

☞ THE FACTS

As well as the sacred ballgame, the Mayas kept their gods happy with gifts of food, drink and objects of gold and silver. The Mayas also carried out human sacrifices because they believed the gods had to be fed with a regular supply of blood.

Mayan nobles used pointed sticks to pierce their ears and tongues in rituals to draw blood for the gods. The most important rituals were carried out by the king. He cut and pierced his body to release blood as a sacrifice.

BALL PLAYER

This stone disc shows a Mayan ball player hitting a ball with his hip. It was made in about CE 591.

The ballgame was popular among peoples throughout Central America. The rules varied between cultures and over time. Even different Mayan cities had their own rules. In general, two teams played on a large stone court with sloping walls. The players used their arms, legs and bodies to move a small rubber ball around the court. They were not allowed to use their hands or feet. In the late Mayan period, after about CE 900, hoops were added to the sides of the court. Players had to get the ball through the hoops to score points.

This illustration recreates a Mayan ballgame.

Spectators stood at the top of the banks on either side of the court.

This large stone disc was found in what is now Chiapas, Mexico. It shows a ballgame player wearing an elaborate headdress.

KINGDOM OF THE MOUNTAINS

The Incas were the first culture to emerge in the Andes Mountains. They settled in the valley of the Urubamba River in around CE **1200** and made Cusco their capital. From there the Incas controlled an empire that stretched the length of the mountain range.

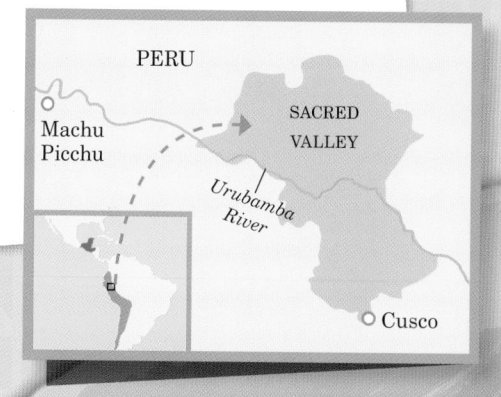

PERU

Machu Picchu

SACRED VALLEY

Urubamba River

Cusco

👉 THE FACTS

- Unlike earlier cultures who had settled on the coast, the Incas settled in the mountains.
- At the empire's greatest extent, in the late fifteenth century, the leaders of the Incas ruled about 12 million people.
- They farmed corn and potatoes on mountainsides, carving terraces into the slopes to grow crops.
- They built a network of roads and bridges to link Cusco with distant parts of the empire.

The Incas called the valley of the Urubamba River the Sacred Valley. The valley was the most important area of farmland in the Inca empire.

LLAMA

The success of the Inca empire was based on efficient transport links.

The Incas build straight roads that made movement around the empire as quick as possible. They built rope bridges over rivers and paved paths across mountain passes. This solid gold figurine is a llama. The Incas used llamas to carry goods through the mountains. The animals are sure-footed, even on steep slopes. The Incas used llama wool to make warm clothes and blankets for the cold winters.

Machu Picchu was a mountain-top city at the head of the Sacred Valley.

This miniature gold llama was made in around CE 1400. Statuettes like this were offerings to the mountain gods.

LAND OF GOLD

In 1532, Spaniards arrived in the Inca capital at Cusco. They could not believe their eyes. The city was full of gold! The Incas used gold to show respect to Inti, the Sun god, because it was the same colour as the Sun.

The Incas built a temple in Cusco dedicated to the Sun god. The temple, called the Temple of the Sun, had gold walls and a garden full of gold statues. Later, the Spaniards built this church on top of the Temple of the Sun.

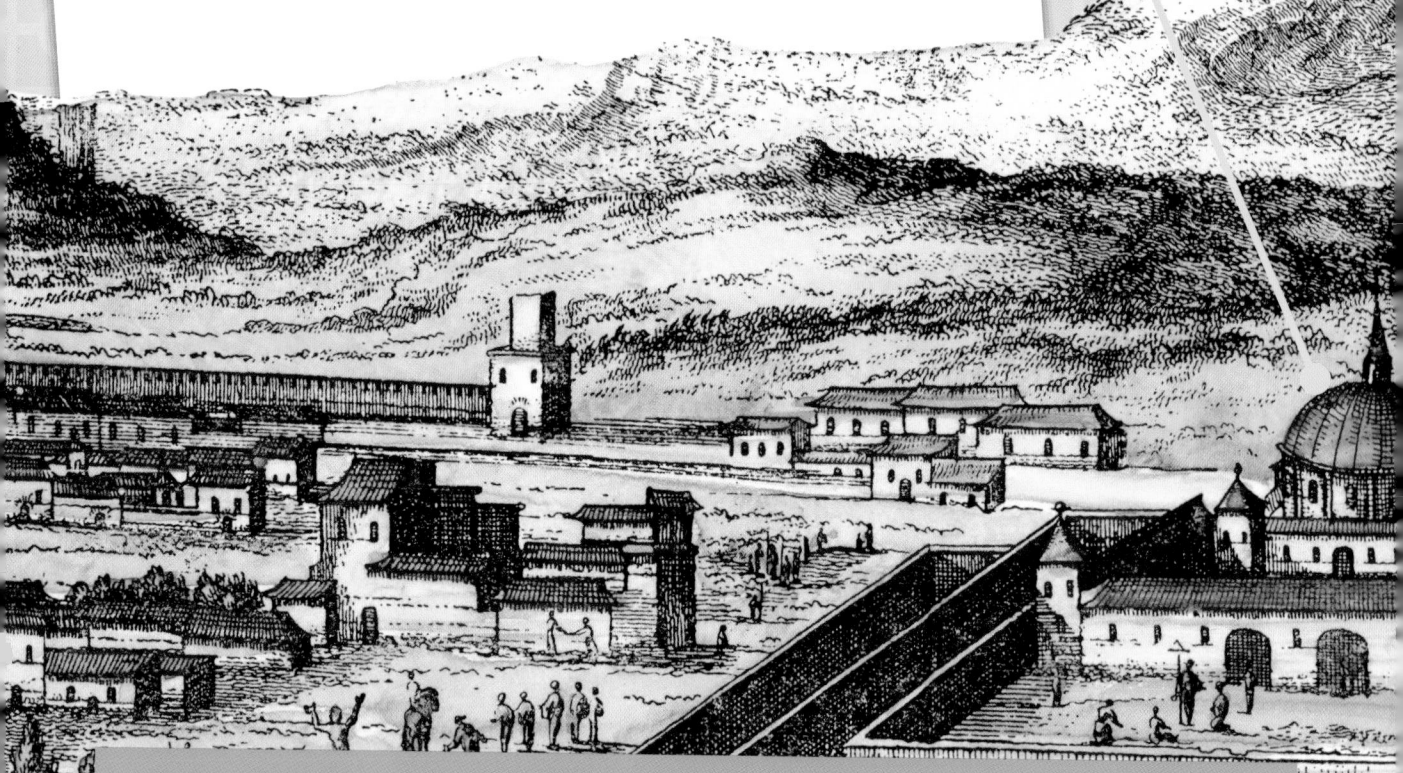

☞ THE FACTS

- The Incas described gold as 'the sweat of the Sun'.
- They called silver 'the tears of the Moon', the goddess Mama Kilya.
- The Incas had plenty of gold and silver, as well as copper and semi-precious stones.

- The Incas did not have to mine for precious metals. Nuggets of gold and silver lay on the ground, and the Incas panned for gold in streams.
- There was no system of money. People paid taxes by working for the empire or with payments of grain.

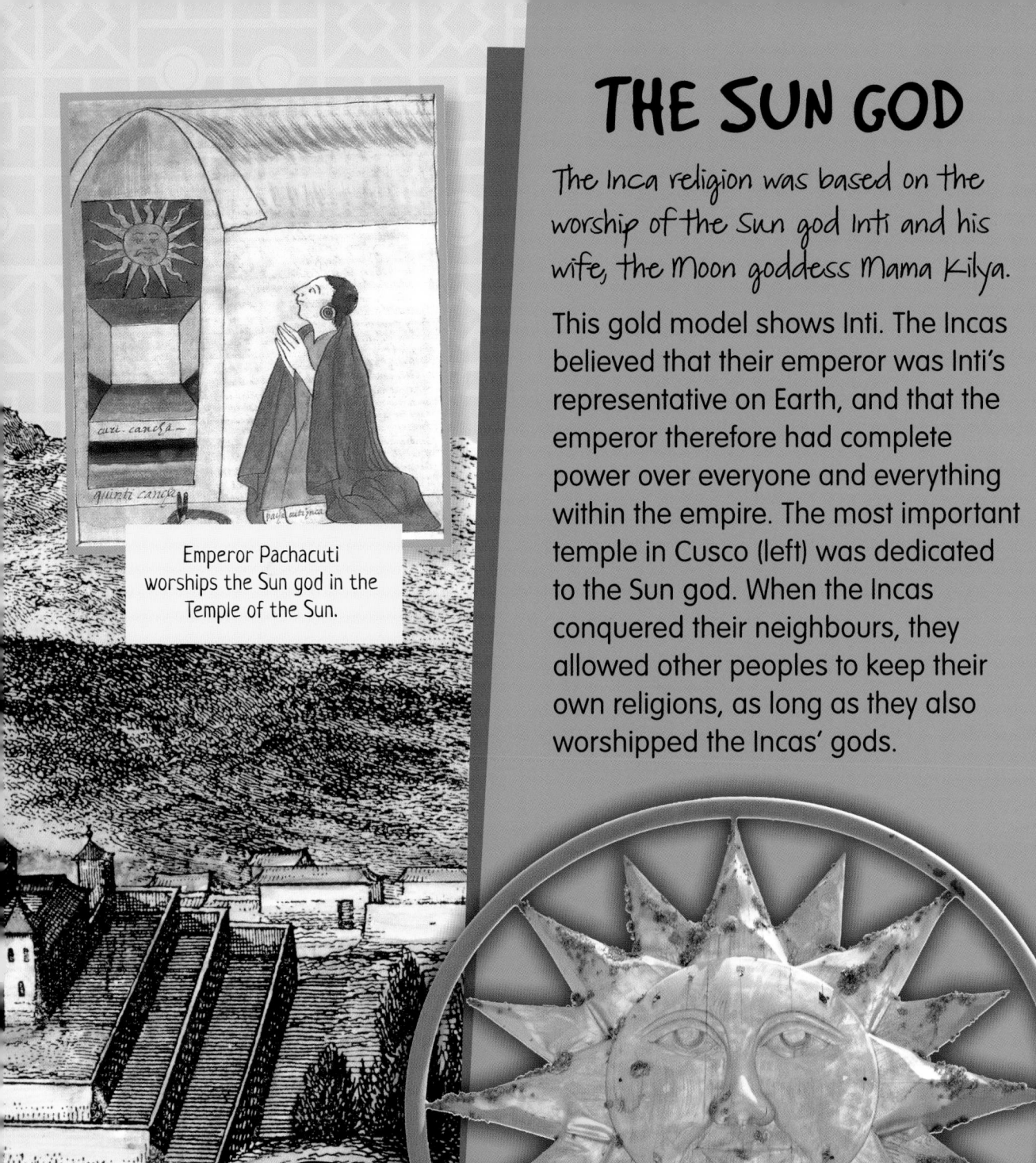

THE SUN GOD

The Inca religion was based on the worship of the Sun god Inti and his wife, the Moon goddess Mama Kilya.

This gold model shows Inti. The Incas believed that their emperor was Inti's representative on Earth, and that the emperor therefore had complete power over everyone and everything within the empire. The most important temple in Cusco (left) was dedicated to the Sun god. When the Incas conquered their neighbours, they allowed other peoples to keep their own religions, as long as they also worshipped the Incas' gods.

Emperor Pachacuti worships the Sun god in the Temple of the Sun.

Depictions of Inti showed him as a face in the Sun surrounded by golden rays.

BUILDING SKILLS

The Incas were skilled builders. They built strong walls using huge stone blocks. Although the builders had no mortar to hold stones together, many Inca walls are still standing, despite the earthquakes that occur in the region.

The fortress of Sacsayhuaman still stands outside Cusco. The walls were built in a series of toothlike angles.

☞ THE FACTS

Inca builders did not have strong enough metal tools to cut stone for building. Instead, they used stone tools to shape their building blocks by pounding them into regular shapes. Workmen shaped stones roughly in the quarry, then finished them at the building site.

The builders used grinding stones and sand to polish the surface of the stones. Once the stone had been shaped, it was moved into place using ropes, poles and ramps. Many of the stones had irregular shapes, so fitting them tightly together must have been like doing a 3D jigsaw puzzle.

MANY-SIDED STONE

This complex stone block forms part of a sacred temple complex in the Inca city of Machu Picchu.

The stone forms part of one wall of a three-sided structure that archaeologists think may have been the Temple of the High Priest. The stone has been shaped so that it has 32 different corners. In Cusco, a famous stone on Hatun Rumiyoc Street (left) has twelve angles. That stone slab formed part of the wall of an Inca palace, which still stands. The stone fits its space so well that it is impossible to slip a piece of paper between it and its neighbours.

Descendants of the Incas sit on an Inca stone wall in Cusco.

The Spaniards noted that the stone blocks were so huge and fitted so well it was as if they were not made by humans.

This stone was part of a temple at Machu Picchu.

CORN

Inca farmers produced enough food to feed everyone in the empire. The empire had four climate zones, including mountains and rain forests, and each zone was suited to growing different crops. The staple crop was corn (maize), which grew well at altitude. The Incas believed corn was sacred. They held a special ceremony when the emperor ploughed the first cornfield of the year with a golden plough.

Farmers used irrigation to grow corn on terraces high above the Sacred Valley.

☞ THE FACTS

- Every Inca family belonged to a community, or *ayullu*, that grew its own food. Each *ayullu* gave part of its crop to the empire as a form of taxation.
- The Incas built canals and cisterns to irrigate the mountainside terraces.
- They dried and stored staple crops such as corn, potatoes and quinoa to use in the winter.
- The Incas built large granaries throughout the empire to store produce to distribute to the people.

SILVER CORN

Corn was easy to grow and had many different uses.

In Cusco, the Incas planted a 'garden' with gold and silver corn stalks like this one. Corn was so important that the Incas believed it was a sacred gift from the gods. Its kernels were dried and then ground to make corn flour that was used to make corn cakes. Popcorn was a popular treat. Fermented corn kernels could be used to make beer, which was used in Inca religious ceremonies.

The Incas grew corn in a range of different varieties and colours.

These silver corn cobs were made between about 1440 and 1553. They are life-sized but hollow.

RUNNING THE EMPIRE

The Incas called their empire Tawantinsuyu, which means the 'Land of Four Quarters'. It was highly centralised. Everything was run from the capital, Cusco. The government made sure everyone paid taxes and, in return, that everyone had enough food.

☞ THE FACTS

The Incas called their ruler *sapa*, which means 'sole ruler'. They believed he was a god on earth. Below the emperor was a group of nobles. The nobles ran the empire and served as priests and warriors. They built a network of roads that spread out from Cusco to carry orders and gather records throughout the empire. Most Incas were peasants and farmers. They paid a tax to the empire known as *mit'a* or tribute. The tax took the form of labour, time or food. The Incas kept records of *mit'a* and other information using knotted strings called *quipu*.

An Inca road zigzags up a mountainside. The roads were built primarily for *chasquis* to use. *Chasquis* were couriers who carried messages rapidly throughout the empire using a relay system.

QUIPU

The Incas had no kind of writing. Instead, they kept detailed records by using quipus. The different colours of string and sizes of knots had specific meanings.

The Inca kept all kinds of records with *quipus*. One bundle of strings might hold as many as 2,000 knots. These knots recorded the population of the empire, together with the amount of tax due from each community. The Inca also kept military information and the dates of important religious ceremonies in *quipus*. Although experts know what the *quipus* were used for, they have not worked out how to read them.

As the supreme ruler of the empire, the Inca emperor was carried around to inspect his lands.

This *quipu* was found in an agricultural storehouse in Peru. It may have recorded the contents of the store.

THE LOST INCA CITY

The Incas built Machu Picchu high in the mountains. After the Spaniards conquered the Incas in 1532, they destroyed most Inca buildings. However, they did not find Machu Picchu. Local people showed the stone walls to the American explorer Hiram Bingham in 1911.

BRAZIL

PERU

Machu Picchu

SOUTH AMERICA

Pacific Ocean

ARGENTINA

☞ THE FACTS

- Machu Picchu is located high above the Urubamba River at the head of the Sacred Valley, 80 kilometres from Cusco.
- The purpose of the city is not fully understood, but it may have been a religious sanctuary.
- It was probably built around CE 1450 and abandoned when the Spanish conquistadors arrived.
- The city was home to stone palaces, temples and houses, with terraces for growing crops and granaries to store corn.

HITCHING POST

Machu Picchu seems to have been the site of rituals intended to make sure the Sun stayed in the sky.

The Intihuatana stone in Machu Picchu is also known as the Hitching Post of the Sun. The Incas believed that this four-sided sacred stone held the Sun in place. They carried out ceremonies at the stone on the two equinoxes, 21 March and 21 September, when day and night are equal length. At midday on those two days the Sun is directly above the stone, so its pillar does not cast a shadow. Nobles and priests carried out rituals to ensure that the bond between Earth and the Sun was not broken.

Hiram Bingham was led to Machu Picchu by local guides.

The city only had homes for a small population. Experts think it was a sanctuary for nobles only.

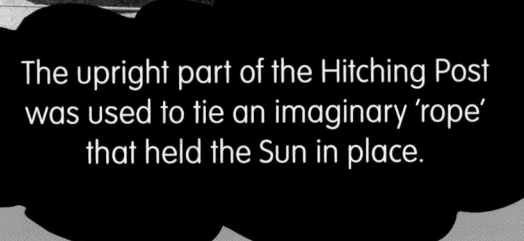

The upright part of the Hitching Post was used to tie an imaginary 'rope' that held the Sun in place.

THE CREATION OF THE
CORN PEOPLE

Just as artefacts tell us a lot about cultures from the past, the stories people told reveal what they thought about their world. Most ancient cultures used myths to explain their beliefs. This story was told by the Mayas.

This carving depicts the Mayan corn god.

When the world began, there were no people, no animals, no flowers or trees. All that existed was the sky, the earth, the oceans and the gods. A plumed serpent, the god Gucumatz, lived at the bottom of the ocean. The sky god Huracan lived in the heavens, where bolts of lightning shot from his head. These two gods decided to create a world. As they discussed this new world, mountains rose from the sea and forests covered the earth.

Next, the two gods created animals. The gods wanted the animals to thank them, but all their creations could do was grunt and squeak. What the gods needed was a creature who would rule over the other animals and thank the gods properly with offerings and prayers. They decided to create humans.

The first human was made from clay. Although he could speak, he talked nonsense. The clay soon disintegrated and the human fell apart. The two gods broke up their creation and started again.

The next human was made from wood. The world quickly filled up with wooden men, but they were rude and had no emotions. The wooden men were so ungrateful they would not even thank their creators. The gods decided to destroy them. They sent a huge flood that washed the wooden men away.

Finally, the other gods advised Gucumatz and Huracan to make four new men out of corn. These new humans were not like the previous ones. They were intelligent and they were grateful to the gods. Now the gods worried that these creatures were too smart. They took away some of their intelligence and replaced it with happiness in the form of four women. The four corn men and four corn women are the ancestors of the whole human race.

TIMELINE OF THE MAYAS AND INCAS

c.600 BCE
The first settlement is built at Tikal. Later it becomes a powerful city-state.

CE 925
Chichén Itzá emerges as a major power on the Yucatan Pensinsula of Mexico.

c. CE 560
Tikal is defeated by an alliance of other city-states.

c.1000 BCE
The Mayas begin to live in large settlements in Chiapas, Mexico.

c.100 BCE
The Mayas build their first pyramids.

1000s BCE	500s BCE	CE 100s	CE 900s

c.700 BCE
The first Mayan writing begins to appear.

c. CE 250
Start of the Classical Period, the peak of the Mayan culture.

c. CE 900
Collapse of Mayan culture in the south marks the end of the Classical Period.

CE 615
Pakal the Great becomes king of Palenque. He rules during the city's golden age.

c. CE 1250
The Mayas abandon the city of Chichén Itzá.

CE 1471
Tupac becomes Inca emperor and begins a huge expansion of the empire.

CE 1517
Spaniards arrive in the Mayan lands, marking the end of the Mayan culture.

CE 1525
The death of Huayana Capac starts a civil war, at the end of which Atahualpa becomes emperor.

CE 1200s	CE 1400s	CE 1500s

c. CE 1200
Manco Capac, the first Inca ruler, founds Cusco in the Andes Mountains.

CE 1493
Huayana Capac becomes Inca emperor. He expands the empire to its greatest extent.

CE 1572
The Spaniards kill the last Inca emperor, Tupac Amaru. This is the end of the Inca Empire.

CE 1438
The Incas begin to expand their control beyond Cusco.

CE 1532
Spaniards arrive in Cusco. The following year they kill Atahualpa.

GLOSSARY

altitude the height of the ground above sea level

archaeologists people who study old ruins and objects to learn about the past

artefacts things that are made by people, particularly in the past

astronomers people who study the movement of bodies in the night sky

centralised controlled from a single location

cisterns tanks for storing water

city-state a political unit formed by a city and its surrounding land

conquistadors Spanish for 'conquerors', Spanish adventurers who went to the Americas in the 1500s, mainly looking for wealth

couriers people who carry messages and packages

fermented affected by living organisms such as yeast that produce alcohol

granaries buildings for storing grain

indigenous relating to the original inhabitants of a place

irrigate to artificially water land in order to grow crops

lintels horizontal supports along the tops of doors and windows

llama a long-necked, four-legged mammal related to the camel

mortar a mixture of sand, water and cement used to fix bricks or stones in walls

nobles members of the elite class of society

nuggets naturally occurring lumps of pure gold or silver

panned separated gold from river mud by rinsing it in a pan of water

quarry a place where stone is dug out of the ground

quinoa (KEEN-wah) a plant whose seeds are used for food

relief carvings carvings that leave details raised above the level of a flat surface

rituals solemn ceremonies that follow a series of actions

sacred connected with a god or gods

sacrifices the giving of something valuable to the gods

sanctuary a place of refuge

sarcophagus a stone coffin, which is often decoratively carved

staple crop an important crop, producing much of the food

terraces flat steps cut into a slope

tribute a payment made to a ruler

FURTHER RESOURCES

Books

History Detective Investigates Mayan Civilization, Clare Hibbert
(Wayland, 2017)

History in Infographics The Mayans, Jon Richards
(Wayland, 2016)

Great Civilisations The Maya, Tracey Kelley
(Franklin Watts, 2015)

Technology in the Ancient World The Maya and Other American Civilisations,
Charlie Samuels
(Franklin Watts, 2015)

Eyewitness Aztec, Inca and Maya
(Dorling Kindersley, 2011)

Websites

www.bbc.co.uk/education/clips/zsdrqty
This BBC site has a short video introducing students to the
civilisation of the Mayas.

www.dkfindout.com/uk/history/mayans/
This page about the Mayas has links to information about many aspects
of their lives and why the civilisation ended.

www.dkfindout.com/uk/history/incas/
This page about the Incas is intended to help students
with study projects.

www.fun-facts.org.uk/wonders_of_world/machu-picchu.htm
This page has many fun facts about the Inca city of Machu Picchu
intended to help with homework.

INDEX